The Dating Game Killer

Life of Serial Killer Rodney James Alcala

Jack Smith

ISBN: 9781730930546

Printed in the United States of America

Cover image credit: by San Quentin State Prison, California Department of Corrections and Rehabilitation - Public Domain, https://commons.wikimedia.org/w/index.php?curid=12864184

MAPLEWOOD
— PUBLISHING —

www.maplewoodpublishing.com

Contents

Introduction

The history of Rodney Alcala is an interesting one. This is a man who had a rough childhood. His father had abandoned them and he had lost a grandmother he was close to. But despite all of this Alcala seemed to be a model student and capable of handling any task that he was given. But despite all of this, things would soon go south for Alcala. This book is going to spend some time looking at the life of Alcala and learning how he became known as the Dating Game Killer.

We'll begin with a brief summary of Rodney Alcala's early life. A person's earliest experiences in infancy and childhood can have a major effect on their later attitudes and actions. So this is a good starting point to better understand Alcala's motivations and the forces that drove him. After a gritty and difficult childhood, Alcala continued into young adulthood with a stint in the military that ended badly. This could have been the beginning of a downhill slide for Alcala that ended in tragedy for his victims.

While Alcala was attending UCLA, he committed his first crimes. His first victim was a young girl only 8 years old. The murders kept on coming and Alcala had many victims in 1977 alone. Of course, during this time, the police did not know Alcala was the one committing them, this wasn't proven until DNA evidence became prevalent many years later, and so Alcala was able to roam about free. Alcala often used the promise of becoming a model and becoming famous to get women to take pictures with him.

During his life, Alcala became known as the Dating Game Killer. While he didn't actually kill anyone during his time on the dating game, he was a contestant on one of the episodes, and actually won a date. This caused a lot of people to associate Alcala with the Dating Game.

Eventually, Alcala was caught and DNA was used to identify him as the killer in many unsolved cases. He has been tried, found guilty and sentenced to death more than once yet still remains incarcerated to this day. Alcala spent many years murdering the women he met. Despite all the evidence pointing at him, including DNA evidence once it became available, Alcala has avoided the death penalty for many years.

To learn more about this fascinating man and all that occurred during his life, including how he was able to stay out of jail for so long, take a look through this book.

The Childhood and Young Adult Life of Rodney Alcala

Rodrigo Jacques Alcala Buquor is a riveting individual who has caught the attention of the media and many others for years.

Rodney Alcala, born August 23, 1943 in San Antonio, Texas, started life differently than the rest of us. Alcala's father, Raoul Alcala Buquor, abandoned the family when Rodney was young, and they never heard from him again. After his father left, Alcala's mother, Anna Maria Gutierrez decided to move the whole family to Los Angeles when Rodney was 12 years old.

Rodney mostly received his education from Catholic institutions. His first school was St. Joseph Catholic Elementary school and then he moved on to Mount Sacred Heart. Despite being prestigious schools in the area, Alcala was able to maintain good grades and he was considered a serious learner. Those who knew him stated he was kind and respectful, and he was never in trouble with behavioral or other issues during school.

In 1951, Alcala's grandmother became ill. She wished to move back to Mexico and finish out her life in her country. To help out, Alcala's mother moved the family as well, forcing the children into a new lifestyle. The Alcala children were used to living in a city and being around a lot of people. In Mexico, they were in a rural area. Alcala continued his education while in Mexico at the American School and continued to excel.

Two significant events occurred during Alcala's time in Mexico. First, his grandmother died. During this period, Alcala had grown close to his grandmother and this was a hard blow to the family. Years earlier Alcala's father had run away and headed back to the states. While these were both traumatizing events, Alcala remained strong, on the outside, and took the events in stride.

After his grandmother's death, Alcala's mother decided to move the family back to Los Angeles so they could start fresh. In 1954, Alcala enrolled in St. Alphonsus and attended for two years. His high school years were spent at Cantwell-Sacred Heart of Mary. Even though Alcala was done with his education and had spent the majority of his time in private schools, he decided during his last semester that he wanted to attend public school. For six months, Alcala went to Montebello High School and graduated in 1960.

Alcala was a social person. He was friends with everyone and often went out on dates or with his friends. He played piano, ran the yearbook planning committee, and was a cross country star. He also had top grades at all the schools he attended.

Rodney joined the U.S. Army in 1960 and became a clerk. He served in this position until 1964 when the army released Rodney from his post because of a nervous breakdown.

Even though Alcala did not show it, he had been deeply affected by the events of his life. But these problems did not show up much until his time in the military. One day about two years into his service, Alcala arrived unexpectedly at his mother's home. He disclosed that he had gone AWOL and was in trouble with the military. His mother tried to convince her son to go back to avoid more trouble from going AWOL. She was surprised that her son, the boy who never got into trouble, had gone AWOL from the military, but hoped they would be able to help him. Alcala went to the local recruiting station and was interviewed by several people, including a psychologist, before being hospitalized and told he needed psychological care. When contacted, Alcala's superiors stated that Alcala seemed off for the past few weeks and had trouble performing his duties during that time.

Alcala was taken to a hospital in San Francisco before being transferred to one in El Toro on a Marine Corps base. Alcala spent some time in this facility while he received the treatment that he needed. After a few months, the military realized that Alcala was not able to perform his standard military duties. He was discharged in 1964 and his treatments stopped at that time.

Many believe this is when things started to go downhill for Rodney Alcala and it may have been part of the reason that he started to become a killer.

This psychiatric diagnosis was not the last time that someone suggested Rodney had mental issues. During his trials, many professionals stated that Rodney has several red flags for personality disorders. Those who evaluated him said that he has borderline personality disorder, narcissistic personality disorder, has issues with sexual sadism comorbidities, and is possibly a psychopath.

Many people wonder why Alcala didn't receive the help that he needed after this evaluation. At the time, the evaluation did not occur until the military dismissed Alcala and it was unlikely that he would seek help on his own. So the issues remained and he was never treated.

After finishing with the Army at 21, Alcala headed off to school. He graduated from the UCLA School of Fine Arts in 1968. Many people liked hanging out with Alcala, and many people wanted to be his friend.

It was also in 1968 that the killer inside him awoke and his murderous activities began.

Tali Shapiro - 1968

Alcala's first victim on September 25, 1968, was Tali Shapiro, a young eight-year-old girl who was on her way to school. At the time, Shapiro lived in Hollywood, California with her family in a hotel since their home had just burned down. The area they moved to, West Hollywood, had a lot of interest for Shapiro, and she would often be late for class because she was so busy exploring all the things that were around her.

On the morning in question, Shapiro was avoiding the bus. She didn't like getting on the bus and riding with the other children; some think she may have been bullied while riding the bus or she could have just enjoyed taking that walk to school. When she left the house that morning, there was no reason for Shapiro to feel like this day would be any different than all the others.

While walking to school, a strange car pulled up next to Shapiro. A younger man peered out the window and asked her if she needed a ride to school. Shapiro had been taught not to talk to strangers by her parents, but the man seemed to know her and her parents, and she was running late for school. So she decided to take the man up on the ride, but she never did arrive at school that day.

Luckily, a witness had seen Shapiro get into the car with an unknown man. Donald Haines was going on a drive down the same street as Shapiro and stopped for a moment at a stop sign. He glanced out of his window and saw a suspicious car that was slowly going along the road while the driver leaned out and talked to a girl. Haines was unsure of whether the girl knew who this man was, but he thought it strange that she barely spoke and kept on walking. After a bit, he noticed that the child got into the car with the man.

Feeling that something was wrong, Haines decided to follow the man. Eventually, the man stopped and got the girl out of the car. Haines, still feeling that something was not right, watched as the girl seemed nervous and hung behind a bit. Feeling that he needed to do something, Haines headed to a pay phone and called the police.

A few minutes later, a patrol car arrived at the scene. The first officer, Officer Camacho, had gone up to the apartment first to try and talk to the man inside and see if this was something to be worried about or not. Camacho stated that he felt a bit weird about the guy, but let him go to get dressed. He claimed he had just gotten done with a shower. Hearing some groaning noises in the house, Camacho, as well as the backup crew, pushed open the door and forced their way into the house.

What they found there was a grisly scene. Young Shapiro, who had been raped and beaten with a steel pipe, lay on the floor barely conscious. Police were able to get her medical attention right away, and over time, she was able to go back home with her parents. Luckily for the girl, her injuries healed and she was knocked out before some of the worst parts of her attack, saving her from these nightmares.

No matter how much the police looked, they were not able to find Alcala in the home. When the officer left him alone for a few minutes, it appears that Alcala was able to escape from his apartment and wasn't seen again for some years.

Shapiro's family then decided that they were going to leave the country. Tali's father left his job in the music industry and moved the whole family to Puerto Vallarta, Mexico. The family hoped this move would give them some peace from the horrible tragedy that had taken place.

Alcala in New York – 1968-1971

Since the authorities never found Alcala in his apartment after the attack, he became a fugitive. The FBI placed Alcala on their most wanted list, and these signs went up all across the country.

After escaping from this arrest, Alcala ran off to New York and changed his name to John Berger. He quickly applied to the School of Arts at New York University. Even though he was a few weeks late in the semester, he was admitted to the film program under Roman Polanski.

Alcala, under the alias of Berger, was well liked. He had a lot of friends, enjoyed doing group projects, and even got to work on a few film crews. Alcala was good looking and even had a few dates during this time. When he wasn't working or at school, Alcala headed out to the Village in the hopes of meeting performers and others into the art and music of the time. He still kept up his high-grade point average.

After spending a bit of time working hard in the film program, Berger decided it was time to take a break from all this activity. Berger decided to take a summer counselor job he was offered at an arts camp for children in New Hampshire. Despite his history of underage sexual assault he managed to get the job. At the time, the employer did not check employee backgrounds and with the alias, Alcala was able to stay on for four years.

While he had no experience in this arena, he was charismatic, and no one had reason to suspect his past crimes. He was easily able to get letters of recommendation and his attendance at New York University (he didn't put UCLA because of the name change) helped him to get this job. In the summer of 1969, Alcala arrived at camp and began his duties.

According to the staff there, Alcala was great at the job. He got along well with both the children and the staffers. He was great at teaching, and the campers loved hearing his stories. He finished out the year before heading back to school, but before leaving, he accepted a job as a counselor for the next summer.

In June 1971, Alcala received his diploma with honors from NYU. He returned for a third summer to the camp in New Hampshire to finish this out before beginning his career as a photographer.

Cornelia Crilley - 1971

During that summer, he committed his second crime, against Cornelia Crilley. Cornelia Crilley had grown up in New York with two brothers, two sisters, and her parents. She had a pleasant childhood, growing up in an Irish neighborhood. Crilley graduated from All Saints Commercial High School in 1965 and took a few clerical jobs to help her pay for flight attendant training.

She took jobs where she could find them, including one at a law office where she found her boyfriend at the time, Leon Borstein. Once she saved up enough money, Crilley went off to Overland Park, Kansas to attend training to become a flight attendant. After she graduated, she came back to New York City and stayed in an apartment with two other flight attendants to save money.

On the day in question, Crilley had been talking to her mother early in the day. Crilley and her roommates had just moved into a new apartment, and she was giving her mother the new address. Mrs. Crilley had to go out but promised to call her daughter back in just a few hours. But when Mrs. Crilley called again, no one picked up. Assuming her daughter had just run out for a bit, she tried again later, but still no answer. Mrs. Crilley continued calling for a few more hours but was not able to reach her daughter.

Worried, Mrs. Crilley called Borstein, explaining her concerns. Figuring Crilley was just out shopping or doing other chores, Borstein promised Mrs. Crilley he would check up on her as soon as he got back to the city. When Borstein finally got done with work that night, he headed over to his girlfriend's house, along with a few police officers just to be safe; everyone assumed miscommunication was to blame.

Borstein got to the apartment and noticed the door was locked. One of the officers went up the fire escape and broke a window to get in. Everything looked normal throughout the house until they entered the second bedroom. Inside, they found a body, partially clothed, lying on the floor. The woman had her upper garments stuffed into her mouth, and her body and face were bruised and beaten. Authorities believed the attacker had sexually attacked the woman as well.

The news of this attack quickly took the area by storm. Several companies and individuals offered rewards for information that would lead to an arrest in the murder, including $100 offered by the Professional Airline Stewardess Association. Some believed that Crilley had only asked someone for help with moving items, and the attack happened at that time. Those that knew Crilley didn't see this as a possibility; they believed that she knew the assailant before letting them in.

Her murder remained unsolved until 2011 when John Berger (Alcala) was indicted.

Later that summer two of the campers at the camp where Alcala worked headed into town to mail off some letters to their parents. The local post office was just a short walk from the camp, so they got permission and took notes for other campers as well. While at the post office, they spent some time looking around, waiting for the rain to stop. It was at this point when they noticed the poster.

Right up on the wall in the post office was the FBI's Ten Most Wanted Fugitives List. They looked at the pictures and the crimes of each one, adding in their comments. All of a sudden, they came across a face that looked familiar.

The man known as Alcala looked just like their camp counselor John Berger. Though they were uncertain if this was the same man, the name was different, and the crime occurred in California while they were in New Hampshire, they went to their director to share the information.

The director went to look up the information as well, figuring there was some mistake, and the girls were just pulling a trick. When he realized the picture was the same, he called the FBI. The agent on the phone told him to act as normal as possible when he arrived back at camp, and FBI would come in the morning. The director told the girls to keep quiet and acted as if nothing were wrong.

Early the next morning, FBI officers came to the camp and took Alcala into custody. After doing a fingerprint test, it was determined that John Berger was Rodney Alcala. Within a short amount of time, Alcala was sent back to California to await his trial for the Shapiro case years before.

Shapiro Trial and Julie J.
1971-1977

While prosecutors were ready to begin the Shapiro trial, it was over before it began. Shapiro now lived with her parents in Mexico, and they refused to come back to testify against Alcala. Without the primary witness, prosecutors were not able to convict Alcala, and they allowed Alcala to plead guilty to assault for which he spent three years in prison. In 1971 Alcala was able to convince the parole panel that he was cured

Alcala was free on parole and went to live with his mother. He took a few weeks to get comfortable living in the new location and out of prison before he began to look for a job. With his dynamic personality, Alcala was able to get a job with a photography company using his education from NYU. For the next few months, he showed up faithfully to work on time and did well on the job.

In mid-October of 1974, Alcala started to get into trouble again. On that day, he was cruising around and pulled into a local shopping center. Across the way, he saw a young girl of eight years waiting to go to school. Seeing her name on the books she carried, Alcala called out directly to her on the bus. Alcala asked if she needed a ride to school. At first, the girl, known later as Julie, ignored Alcala. When the girl would not go with Alcala, he turned on the charm. He promised he would take her to see some amazing posters, and she would still be on time to school. Julie finally agreed it would be more fun to get a ride to school rather than riding the bus.

The two started to talk, but soon Julie felt that something was not right. Her suspicions were verified when the man went right past her school and would not stop. Julie began to fidget and would not sit still. The man got angry with her and started to get violent. When the vehicle stopped, Julie attempted to run away, but the man would not let her go; instead, he led her up to the cliffs, fifteen minutes from the bus stop.

Once they were on the bluff, the man forced Julie to sit down before giving her marijuana she had to take. Out of fear, Julie smoked the marijuana before trying to escape again. The man grabbed her again and began making out, asking if she was interested in sex.

Just a few yards down the cliff, a park ranger was taking a walk on the trails. He happened to look up at the spot where these two were located and saw two people in a location where they were not supposed to be. The ranger caught both of them with the pot and decided to arrest them until the story was figured out. Alcala claimed that Julie had brought the marijuana for both of them to use while Julie claimed that she had been kidnapped and brought to the area against her will.

The police pulled background checks on both Alcala and Julie. Julie's record came back clean, but since Alcala gave his real name, his long criminal history, including that he was a parolee, came back. Shortly afterward, Alcala was brought before a judge and faced several charges including violating his parole, kidnapping, and sale of pot.

Though Alcala ended up in prison again, he remained for just 34 months. The "indeterminate" sentencing program, an idea that was popular at the time, allowed offenders to receive release once they showed rehabilitation.

This time around, Alcala served his prison time starting in Chino before being moved to the California's Men's Colony in San Luis

Obispo. This second location was meant to provide Alcala with the rehabilitation that he needed. But by this time, Alcala had become a master of fooling people. In a short amount of time, Alcala showed self-improvement and in 1977, the parole board declared that Alcala was rehabilitated and safe to come back into society. There was one condition that Alcala must face when the board released him; he had to visit each week with his parole officer.

For some time, Alcala reported each week to his parole officer. Then one day, Alcala made a plea to the police to go to New York to visit with some relatives. He promised the trip would be short, just a few days. The parole officer agreed to this short trip, thinking that Alcala had made the correct changes in prison to be safe for society.

In July of 1977, just a month after he received parole, Alcala again headed off to New York. Despite all the warning signs and his past behavior, everyone seemed fine with Alcala heading out across the country. Allowing Alcala to leave the state proved to be a very dangerous idea for the young man, and his victims, for some time to come.

Ellen Hover - 1977

Ellen Jane Hover was the next victim claimed by Alcala. Hover was a 23-year-old woman who had just graduated from Beaver College in Pennsylvania. She was a Biology major with a minor in music. Since Hover was a small-town girl and had gone to college in a rural area, she was excited to start out in the big city. Hover was known around as a young socialite thanks to her father, Herman Hover; Herman was the owner of the legendary Ciro's nightclub in Hollywood, the same club where Dean Martin, Lucille Ball, Mickey Rooney, and all the famous celebrities in Hollywood hung out. Hover had grown up with wealth and privilege, but she was also a bit sheltered and knew everyone around her.

Thanks to her advanced degree, her status, and her wealth, Hover was able to get a great start in the city. She found an apartment in an excellent location that was also close to her mother. Authorities believe that the first time Hover met Alcala was in July of 1977, right after he came back to New York. On that night, a friend who lived in the same apartment building noticed her chatting with an unknown man and asked Hover about it. Hover explained that he was a photographer, and dropped the conversation.

On July 15, Hover headed out early in the morning to explore the city and get some errands done. She came back in time to have a quick lunch with the same man for a few nights before he showed up again and knocked on her door. That evening, Hover missed out on a dinner date with her friend.

Missing appointments was uncharacteristic for Hover, who always kept her appointments and loved going out with friends. She also did not call her parents, a tradition she had started each night at college. When her mother tried to call Hover, there was no answer.

By mid-morning, her friends and family began to worry a bit. Hover hadn't contacted anyone at all since the day before, and she wasn't answering her phone. Feeling that they were overreacting, but wanting to play it safe, her mother and stepfather called the police. The police went over to Hover's apartment to see if anyone was there. They didn't notice any signs of a break-in and got permission to enter the house from her mother. Nothing in the house seemed unusual.

The one thing that stood out to police was the open diary on her end table. It was open to an appointment for the day before. The date only said "John Berger, photographer." This information wasn't much, but this, at least, gave the investigators a place to start.

Hover's wealthy family offered a reward to anyone who could provide information that led to their daughter's discovery. Ruben Schwartz, Hover's stepfather, offered $100,000 to find his stepdaughter and even went as far as to hire a private investigator in the hopes of finding her again.

The private investigator did help the investigation along a bit. After a few days, they reported back that John Berger was a ponytailed photographer who had been seen outside Hover's apartment several times before. Schwartz placed ads in the New York Times to see if anyone had information about Berger. No one ever came up with any information.

Despite Hover having a high position in society at the time, there were many deaths going on in the city during this period, and without a body and very little to go on, they weren't able to find Hover at that time.

The FBI called the LAPD because of their investigation into the disappearance of Ellen Hover. The FBI wanted to find a John Berger, the name that was in Hover's diary on the day she disappeared. Through preliminary research, the FBI found that John Berger was an alias that Rodney Alcala used and that Alcala lived in LA.

The LAPD was able to find Alcala in no time. They still had him registered in the state and were able to bring him in for questioning. During this time, investigators told Alcala about Ellen Hover and how she had gone missing from New York City. They asked Alcala if he was able to shed some light on the situation.

Alcala surprised the investigator by admitting that he did know Hover and had been with her for a bit on the day. He claimed that he met Hover one day while taking photos in New York. The two had discussed meeting to take some pictures but promised that he had no idea what happened once the two came back home.

Feeling that something was wrong, the authorities asked Alcala to take a polygraph test. Alcala refused, and the police had to let him go. They still didn't have a body or any evidence other than the two had met, so they were not able to hold him.

Hover's case went cold and was not concluded until 2011.

By this point, Alcala was becoming a master at killing women and not having authorities catch him. He had gotten away with a few murders without anyone finding him. Even when police did catch Alcala, he received minimal sentences, often not for the crime he committed.

After killing Hover, Alcala stayed around New York City for some time before returning to California.

California - 1977

After spending about a month in New York, Alcala came back to Los Angeles and decided to start out on a new career path. He applied for work as a typesetter for the Los Angeles Times. Despite having a long criminal history, Alcala was given the job and got started right away. He quickly charmed everyone he met at work and liked to share stories and stay late to get work done.

Meanwhile, many unsolved murders were occurring in the area. The Hillside Strangler Task Force interviewed Alcala as a potential suspect, but they quickly ruled him out. Alcala was not able to stay out of trouble though. During his time at the Los Angeles Times, he was arrested and spent some time in jail for marijuana possession.

Once Alcala was released, it seemed that he was back on the right path. He retained the job with the Los Angeles Times as a typesetter and concentrated on his photography.

Alcala started to change his personality. He convinced hundreds of women and men that he was a professional photographer and added them to his portfolio. Many of the models were naked; they agreed to do the shoot because Alcala claimed to be a professional and the models wanted to become famous. Alcala had many pictures of naked teenage boys as well as girls and most of these were sexually explicit pictures. While many of the models are unidentified, authorities worry that some may be cold case victims.

It was during this time that Alcala met Sharon Gonzales. Gonzales was a fellow employee who quickly became impressed with Alcala. She loved all of the stories about his time in

Hollywood and New York and his charm immediately intrigued her. The two began a friendship while at work.

Over time, Alcala began to show her some of his portfolio, mostly nudes of young girls. Showing these pictures became a practice that he began doing with many people at work. Some found it a bit strange to see this portfolio, but Alcala stated that the parents of the girls asked him to take the pictures.

Despite all the weird images, most of his coworkers liked Alcala. He had a natural personality that they all could talk to and he did his job well. None of them knew about his shady past and all felt that he was a great addition to the team. This portfolio would only continue to grow over the years. Later on, investigators would release the pictures in hopes of family members recognizing some of them and offering some closure to cold cases.

Jill Barcomb - 1977

Jill Barcomb was born in 1958 and was the fifth child in the Barcomb family. She lived with her large family in the area of Oneida, New York. They were a very devoted Catholic family, spending each Sunday in church and then saying their prayers each night before bed. While Jill considered herself happy in this family life and loved having lots of brothers and sisters around, by the time she turned 17, she was ready to head out on her own and explore the world. She dropped out of school during her senior year.

Jill's parents did not approve of the new ways that Jill was taking. They felt that she should go back to school and finish her education. Instead, Jill moved out of the home and lived with her older sister Debbie for some time. After a few months, Jill and a few friends decided to get in a van and start heading out to LA to try something new.

When Jill headed out west, she did not tell her family of her plans right away. The fact that Jill didn't tell anyone about her plans to leave made some worry as no one knew where she was. About a week afterward, Jill finally called her family to tell them about going to California. She apologized for not letting them know about her plans before she headed out, but she had been worried that they would overreact and not let her go.

In November of 1977, the body of Barcomb was found in West Los Angeles. The authorities found the body on all fours with the toes touching the ground, and the knees point outwards. She suffered from massive neck, head, and face trauma and had blood seepage all around her brain. There were blood vessels in the eye that indicated that the body was deprived of oxygen. The autopsy also found a deep bite mark that was near the right breast and many blood smears and deep scratches all around her body.

For this investigation, authorities looked to see if there were links to the Hillside Strangler. Barcomb had known Judith Miller, a victim of the Hillside Strangler, who had been murdered just a few weeks before. Her remains looked similar to some of the other victims of the Hillside Strangler, and many worried that she was another victim of this same person.

Georgia Wixted - 1977

Georgia Wixted was a young girl around 27 years old at the time of her disappearance. While her family originally came from a small town in New York, they moved to Los Angeles when Georgia was only five. The middle child of a family of three, she was always happy to see people and loved the idea of being there when people needed you most. Because of a medical scare when she was in high school, Georgia spent some time in hospitals in California and New York and soon decided that she wanted to be a nurse when she grew up.

The path to becoming a nurse was not easy for Georgia. Going to medical school is expensive, and her family did not have the money to help her. Feeling like this was still the thing for her to do, Georgia started working as a medical assistant. Working at this job allowed her to help pay for her education and to learn more about the medical field along the way. Her first job out of school was working at Centinela Hospital as a cardiac care nurse.

It was in 1977 when things changed for Georgia unexpectedly. While she had the job of her dreams, a new house, and lots of friends, it all came to a sudden end.

On a typical day, Georgia would often give her coworker, Barbara Gale, a ride to and from work. The two worked the same shift and Georgia went past the area anyway, so it made sense that the two rode together. The day before Georgia disappeared, she had left work at 11:30 p.m. with Gale and went out to a birthday party. Georgia didn't know anyone at the party but hung out with her friend for a bit before they both went home. Gale went to bed early in the morning after making plans for the two to meet up the next day.

The next day, Georgia did not show up. Gale was expecting Georgia to show up by 2:30 p.m., but the time came and went and still Georgia was nowhere to be found. Assuming that Georgia had slept in late, Gale gave her a call to see what was going on. No one answered, despite numerous calls to get hold of her. Gale found another ride to work and found it strange that Georgia was not there nor had she called in sick that day; by this point, Gale was hoping that Georgia had just forgotten to get her. Gale's mother convinced her to call the police to check up on Georgia.

That day, the LAPD went to Georgia's apartment and found her dead inside. There was blood all over the bed, on her clothes, on the floor and everywhere else. The girl looked as though she had been raped as well as beaten with a heavy object. It was a painful sight to see; the family left it up to someone else to help out because they just weren't able to handle the sight. Georgia's mother ended up enrolling in a mental institution because of the nervous breakdown she suffered after hearing of the sad fate of her daughter.

There was a lot of speculation about who may have killed Georgia. She was a young woman who didn't seem to have a lot of enemies in her life. She hung out with a few friends, went to church on the weekends, often saw her family, and went to work. Some wonder if she happened just to cross paths with someone who got mad at her. Others wonder if she met someone at the party and things went south. It would take some time before they were able to find out the real answers for Georgia.

Pamela Lambson - 1977

Pamela Jean Lambson was the only daughter of Jean and Kenneth Lambson. Born in 1958, she was just 19 when she met a handsome photographer at an Oakland A's game who gave her his card and promised to take her picture and make her a star.

Pamela was employed at a local computer company as a secretary but yearned for the bright lights of Hollywood. So, on October 8, 1977, she met the stranger at Fisherman's Wharf in San Francisco. She had always wanted to be an actress and singer so the bright, pretty blonde went off with him and never came home.

Her tortured and battered body was found on a trail on nearby Mount Tamalpais. She was nude and had been sexually assaulted and strangled.

A store clerk had seen Pamela with the stranger and was able to give the authorities a description of the man. Police developed a sketch but were unable to solve the crime.

Years later, another sketch drawn from a description given by another witness to another crime was compared to the 1977 sketch. They are eerily similar. The new sketch had been used to solve the murder of Robin Samsoe. The killer was Rodney Alcala.

Although DNA has not been able to verify it, the authorities are convinced that Pamela Lambson's killer was Rodney Alcala.

Alcala - 1978

Due to all the murders in the area, a special task force had been put together to try and find the Hillside Strangler. They didn't have a ton of leads to go on, but since the suspect had raped all of their victims, they started out with going through all the sex offenders registered in the area. They hoped that this would, at least, lead them on the right path.

During their investigations, the authorities took some time to visit with Rodney Alcala. Thanks to his past issues, he had become a known sex offender in the area. At this time, he was living in Monterey Park in the home of his mother. It wasn't until March of 1978 that the authorities made it to Alcala. The authorities asked to speak with him about the murders and were surprised at how articulate he seemed to be.

Alcala was able to explain his exact location on each day that the crimes had occurred. The interview lasted for a long time and Alcala was able to convince the authorities he was clean in this case. The authorities did see some marijuana in the home and took him to jail because of the drug possession. He only spent a bit of time in prison before being paroled.

Despite all the interviews that went on, the authorities still were not able to find the one responsible for all these deaths. They worried that the suspect would strike again before they could find out whom they were, or that they had somehow missed who was responsible. The search continued.

Authorities were searching all over the area in the hopes of finding who had committed these atrocious murders. Despite the fact that police had cleared Alcala of having anything to do with these killings, they kept on happening. Alcala may have had excuses for where he was each day, but having few friends on the record and living in his mother's house, the woman loved him but didn't keep track of where he was going, made it easy for Alcala to come and go as he pleased.

This lack of attention made it easy for Alcala to get away with whatever he wanted. He often worked out the murders, so he had a witness, at least his mother, for quite a bit of the night. He made short relationships with the girls, usually under the guise of taking pictures. This cover helped him to find a lot of women, in a short amount of time. Whether the girls were aspiring models or were taken in by Alcala's smooth voice or were looking for a few extra bucks, Alcala was able to get an almost endless supply of new girls into his trap.

And Alcala was smooth. Everyone who had been around him at some point or another stated how smooth of a talker he was. It would have been easy for Alcala to get these women to trust him and that would be the last and worst mistake of their lives.

Through this time, the pictures in Alcala's portfolio began to get a bit stranger. He continued to show them off at his job at the Los Angeles Times, and some people felt uncomfortable about it. Alcala assured his coworkers that the parents or the models themselves had asked for and approved the poses. These pictures made the colleagues feel like something was off but still, no one placed him in connection with any of the murders that were going on.

The Dating Game - 1978

Up to this point, Rodney Alcala had been responsible for several murders. While he was only convicted twice, and on lesser charges, he seemed to have found ways to commit more killings over the years without police finding him. But soon Rodney Alcala would become more of a household name, and it would become harder for him to hide away from the public eye.

In September of 1978, Rodney was invited to be on The Dating Game as one of the available bachelors. The producers of the show asked Alcala to appear despite the fact that he had spent time in jail and was registered as a sex offender. Whether the producers didn't do a background check on Alcala before asking him to be on the show, or they felt that enough time had passed since these crimes happened. Either way, Alcala was invited to be on the show and did fairly well.

During his time on the show, he was introduced as a photographer, although this was something that he just did on the side and most people knew nothing about this hidden talent. They went on to state that he had been working in photography since the age of thirteen and that it was his life's passion. He was one of the three bachelors available to choose from on September 13, 1978.

The Bachelorette was Cheryl Bradshaw. Bradshaw was a young woman with dark brown hair, brown eyes, and a big smile for everyone she met. Bradshaw was a teacher from the Phoenix, Arizona area. She was able to ask the bachelor's any question that she liked except what each made, their age, their professions, or their names.

This show was full of sexual innuendos and other phrases that made the audience cheer and clap. Bradshaw seemed to focus most of her attention on Alcala, and they appeared to have a lot of chemistry during the show, at least for the audience to view. When it came time for Bradshaw to pick which bachelor she would like to go on a date with, she chose Alcala over the other bachelors.

The audience loved her choice. Through the show, they had fallen in love with Alcala's charm and how well he answered the questions. When Bradshaw picked Alcala, the camera came right over to him, and he gave off the best performance possible, smiling and looking excited. The audience was told that the two would be heading out for a roller coaster ride at Magic Mountain and tennis lessons for their first date. The audience felt that this was a match that could end in true love, but things did not go as smoothly.

Bradshaw did not feel comfortable going out with Alcala after they met. While they seemed like a good couple on the show, Bradshaw felt that there was something wrong with Alcala. She told others that the man made her feel uncomfortable and like something was off. Some think that Bradshaw was nervous due to the news reports about Jill Barcomb and the other murders in the area. Either way, she refused to go out with Alcala on her own, and the date never happened.

This refusal did not go well with Alcala. He felt that he had rightfully earned the date with Bradshaw. Up to this point, Alcala had been used to getting everything he wanted. He had been able to charm his way out of many predicaments, had an excellent job, and despite his past as a sex offender, he had been invited onto the Dating Show. Everything had always worked out well for Alcala. Even when he ended up in jail, he easily shortened his term up to just a few years rather than a whole decade. Alcala was used to getting what he wanted, and he didn't know how to handle it when things stopped working out for him.

Some psychologists believe this rejection had a profound effect on Alcala. Those with his personality disorders often didn't like it when others stood up to them. They expected everyone to go along with the plans, never deviating. But when Alcala was rebuffed during the Dating Show, it may have set off a reaction since Alcala felt he was treated unfairly.

No matter how Alcala reacted to the rejection, his murder spree didn't end at this point.

Alcala - 1978

Even after his appearance on the Dating Game the year before, Alcala did not seem intent to stop with his killing sprees. At this point, his trouble with the law had been going on for some time. But Alcala had never been put in jail or even brought to trial for these crimes. The few that authorities had connected to him ended up on lesser charges; his first victim, Shapiro, would not come back to America, and so the prosecutors lost their primary witness and Alcala got off with lower charges. The second crime was more about breaking his parole, and he was able to get out of trouble in no time.

The other crimes, no one, had been able to point these crimes back to Alcala. The closest was when authorities came to ask Alcala about the Hillside Strangler victims. Authorities never thought Alcala was responsible for these deaths, though; they only went through their list of registered sex offenders and questioned each one and Alcala happened to be one of them on the list. While investigators spent quite a bit of time interviewing Alcala, his story checked out, and they were all swept away by how charming Alcala seemed while they talked to him.

At one point, another person was placed in jail for the crimes. Alcala was able to go along raping, beating, and murdering more women, and no one seemed interested in checking out this known offender.

Charlotte Lamb - 1978

Charlotte Lamb was a woman of thirty-two years old. She liked to go out and have fun with her friends whenever possible. Lamb was a student at the time and was able to catch the attention of many men thanks to her great figure and blond hair. On the night of June 23, 1978, she had called one of her friends to see if they wanted to check out Moody's, a newer club in the Santa-Monica area. Lamb attended Santa Monica College in the area and was ready to take a night off from studying and have some fun. Her friend declined, stating that he wanted to stay in with his girlfriend that night, but wished her luck while she had fun.

A few days later, Lamb's sister, Celia, called to wish Charlotte a happy birthday, just like she did each year. Lamb didn't answer her phone, and Celia continued to call throughout the day, but no one ever answered. Celia became worried, not only because Charlotte hadn't answered her phone yet, but also because she hadn't heard back about the birthday card that she sent a few days before, something that was unusual for Charlotte.

After some time, Celia got worried and called the authorities. They headed over to Lamb's apartment, sure that there was just some miscommunication, and the young girl would soon show up. They got to the building and asked a manager to let them inside when no one answered them at the door. Detectives walked through the apartment but found that everything was neat and tidy without any issues. After a bit of research, they found that no one had heard from Charlotte for a few days. She hadn't even shown up to work for a few days, something unusual to her character, and her office hadn't been able to locate her. The authorities began to create a profile and look for Lamb.

Soon, Lamb's disappearance became another murder. This one was very bloody and occurred in the laundry room of an El Segundo apartment building in a location south of Lamb's home. They believed that she was either forced or lured to leave Moody's with someone, rather than going back home on her own, and no one ever saw her again.

Finding Ellen Hover - 1978

At about the same time that Lamb had been murdered, the New York City Police located Ellen Hover's body. This revelation was about eleven months after Hover disappeared. Authorities were able to find her skeletal remains in North Tarrytown in Westchester County. Thanks to the identifications on her body, like the ankle bracelet and two rings, and her dental records, authorities were able to prove that these remains were those of Ellen Hover.

The investigators had been able to find Hover thanks to some information they received concerning Alcala. During December 1977, authorities investigated Alcala, who admitted to spending some time with Hover before she disappeared. Feeling that something was still not right about the situation, the authorities started talking to anyone who may have known Alcala when he was in New York.

The authorities received many tips throughout their investigation. First, they found that Alcala was fond of sitting on the Hudson River and watching the sunset from this location. Investigators found a smaller piece of land that had lots of trees near this part of the Hudson River and spent time going through this area to search for evidence. Soon, they found the remains that proved to be Hover.

The news broke out in the area; headlines were on every news channel, and each newspaper had some shocking new secret about this murder. Shortly after this news broke, a single woman from New York called the authorities, stating that she knew Rodney Alcala and that she had been a model for a photo session with him. Authorities quickly brought her in for questioning and hoped this would be the break they needed.

Monique Hoyt - 1979

Monique Hoyt was the next unfortunate victim of Alcala's. She was just fifteen years old when she met Alcala. She lived in Pasadena, which was just outside of the Los Angeles area. On February 13, 1979, Hoyt had been hitchhiking in the area, trying to get to town from her home. It was at this time that a man pulled up right next to her.

Hoyt found this man charming and liked the idea that he asked her to pose for a few photographs. He explained that this was for a contest he was trying to enter, and he continued to talk until Hoyt was so flattered that she agreed to go along to take the pictures. Hoyt was young and had run away from home. This unknown man charmed her and offered her an opportunity she wasn't going to get anywhere else.

Hoyt didn't ask too many questions. She liked how friendly this man was to her, despite her younger age, and she noticed there was a ton of photography equipment in the back of the car. For a young girl, this was all she needed for evidence that this man would help her out.

The couple headed back to Alcala's mother's home, the place where Alcala was living at the time. Alcala explained that he had left a few things back at the house and needed to grab them for the photography session. By the time they got back to the house and grabbed a few things, the sun was setting, and it was too late to take the pictures. Alcala and Hoyt ended up spending the night together at the house.

Early in the morning, Hoyt and Alcala drove to a little-deserted area that was near Banning, around eighty miles from Los Angeles. They stopped at a location that Alcala had described in great detail to Hoyt the day before and she was excited at the prospect of posing for a real photographer. The two got out of the car and started walking away from the road. Alcala made them stop about fifteen minutes away, in a lovely secluded area in the woods.

The two got started right away. At first, Alcala just took pictures of Hoyt, but soon he asked if she would mind doing a few nude shots. She agreed, and they took a few more pictures. Before Hoyt knew what was going on, she felt something big smash into her head. She blacked out and knew nothing more for a time.

A bit later, Hoyt regained consciousness. Having been a runaway for some time and hearing stories about other girls, Hoyt knew that she shouldn't react in a panic right away. She pretended that she was asleep and tried to think of a way to get out of the situation. Then Alcala began his attack. He started to bite her on the breasts and in her genital areas. She tried not to cry out in pain, knowing that this reaction would just anger the man. Alcala continued, first penetrating her in the vagina and then sodomizing her. Finally, Hoyt couldn't take it any longer, and she started to scream.

The screaming angered Alcala, and he stuffed a T-shirt into her mouth while yelling at her to be quiet. Since Hoyt would not stop, Alcala used his hands to choke her until she blacked out again.

A short time later, Hoyt woke up again. She tried to move her feet and hands and noticed that she had been tied up at the ankles and wrists with rope. She wasn't able to move at all. She opened one of her eyes and noticed that Alcala was lying right next to her. Hoyt also noticed a strange sound, as though someone was sobbing. Hoyt decided that instead of panicking, she would try to show concern and see if she could get Alcala to trust her rather than harm her again.

Hoyt started out by telling Alcala how she liked him and how she had enjoyed spending time with him. She rolled over a bit and tried to touch his arms, asking if Alcala was okay after the ordeal. When Alcala didn't answer, Hoyt pleaded with him to not tell anyone what had just happened. She continued to ask if she could go back to his house and if they could go there together.

After a bit of talking, Hoyt seemed to break through to Alcala. Alcala untied the bonds on Hoyt and waited for her to get dressed before the two headed back to the car. The car ride back was silent; Alcala seemed lost in his thoughts and Hoyt worried that saying anything would set him off again. On the drive back to town, Alcala made a stop to use the bathroom, and Hoyt made a run for it.

Hoyt made it to a motel that was right next to the rest stop and started screaming. People in the building heard her, and she asked them to call the police, stating a man had kidnapped and raped her. One of the guests called 911 and other brought Hoyt into the building to wait for the cops. It only took a few minutes for the police to arrive, but in that time, Alcala managed to drive off.

Hoyt agreed to head to the station to answer a few questions. They concentrated on figuring out who the attacker was. The authorities showed Hoyt six pictures based on the description she gave of the man. Hoyt pointed out the one that was Alcala right away. Hoyt was then taken to the hospital to be treated for the minor injuries she had and authorities headed out to visit Alcala.

Alcala was at his mothers' home, seemingly just enjoying the day. When asked about what he had been up to, he stated that he was on parole for marijuana possession but otherwise had just spent his time working and hanging out with some friends. Authorities began to question Alcala about what he had been up to that day. Alcala was not able to come up with a decent alibi, unlike the other times police had come to visit, and authorities read Alcala his rights and put him under arrest for rape. On February 14, Alcala went back to jail.

The story that Alcala provided to authorities was a bit different than what Hoyt told police. According to Don Lasseter in Perfect Justice, Alcala sat down with officials and agreed for them to tape his interview. Alcala stated that Hoyt had gone on a drive with him after agreeing to let Alcala photograph her.

According to Alcala, Hoyt also agreed to simulate some sex acts with him and had even gone as far as being tied up during the session. At one point, Hoyt had begun to struggle with the restraints, and Alcala decided to choke her, so she became unconscious. Alcala also confirmed that he had attempted to stop Hoyt from yelling by stuffing a shirt in her mouth.

Authorities were incredulous at the story Alcala shared. Other than a few things, such as Hoyt agreeing to the sexual acts, the stories were similar. Authorities asked why Alcala would do these things to someone else. He explained how he had panicked and didn't know the right way to react.

A few days later, Alcala was brought before the judge. Prosecutors had requested a bail of $50,000, thinking that Alcala had been a threat to the public before and shouldn't be allowed to roam free until after the trial. The proceeding judge thought differently though and set the bail at $10,000. Alcala's mother paid the bail, feeling that this was a mistake that police would figure out in no time. Police released Alcala on March 16 with a trial set for September.

Just a month after authorities released him from jail, Alcala gave his notice to the Los Angeles Time. He explained that he wanted to start his own photography business and would be devoting his time to working on this rather than his typesetting job. It was more likely that Alcala wanted to get ready for his upcoming trial.

Jill Parenteau - 1979

Jill was the youngest of three children in the Parenteau family. She was quite a bit younger than her older siblings; her siblings were sixteen and six when she was born. But despite the age difference, Jill was able to fit into the family seamlessly, and she grew up looking forward to living the grown-up life that she saw her older siblings enjoying.

At the time in question, Jill had been attending Pasadena City College and studying business. Because of the amount of time she had already spent at the company and her business classes, Jill was offered a management position at her job at Technibilt, Ltd. She lived on her own, but she would go out with some friends several times a week; they would often hang out at the Handlebar Saloon, a bar they had been to many times in the past and with which they were very familiar.

On June 13, 1979, about a month after Alcala put in his notice to the Los Angeles Times, Jill had called her sister. The two talked for a bit, and Jill mentioned that she was going to head out on a date with Dan Brady to the Dodgers game. Jill's sister, Deedee, knew that Brady had had a crush on Jill for many years and was excited that the two were going out. Though Deedee knew that Jill was probably just being friendly, she hoped that the two would hit it off and maybe the relationship would finally go further. This date would be the only date that Brady and Jill ever went on. Jill came home late from the game.

The next day, things were different. Kathy Bowman, a friend of Jill's, called Jill like they did every morning before heading off to work. When Bowman didn't hear from Jill first, she decided to give her friend a call, assuming Jill had gone into work early or had slept in a bit. When Jill didn't answer, Bowman headed off to work, figuring she would talk to her friend later. Later in the day, Bowman gave Jill another call, but when there was still no answer, she called Sandy, Jill's boss, to see if Jill had shown up to work for the day.

This was when the troubling news appeared. Sandy had not heard anything from Jill. This silence was unusual for Jill who always showed up on time, or at least called ahead to explain why she was running later. Sandy assumed Jill would arrive soon, but Bowman felt that something was off and couldn't concentrate on her work. After some time, Bowman called both of Jill's siblings, asking if they had heard from their sister that day. When they hadn't, Bowman decided it was time for someone to check on Jill and see what had happened. Janet Jordan, one of Jill's coworkers, agreed to head over to Jill's apartment and see what was going on.

The scene that greeted Jordan was not a good one. She let herself into Jill's apartment and soon had to call the police over to come to look at the scene. The authorities quickly entered the apartment and noticed that a large window, one with seven panes in it, had been removed, and the screen was cut open so someone could break inside. And someone had unscrewed one of the lightbulbs at the stairwell, probably to make it more difficult for anyone to notice the attacker.

In one of the bedrooms, the police saw the dead body of Jill. She was nude, laying face up right next to the bed. Her legs had been spread open, and the back and shoulders were propped up

48

with some pillows as if the attacker had posed Jill this way. Jill had suffered trauma to the head, teeth, cheeks, and nose with ligature marks all over her and authorities believe that the attacker strangled her to death.

Without DNA evidence, it was difficult for police to determine who had committed this crime. The family and friends of Jill felt that this was a heinous crime done by a monstrous person. Some wondered if Brady might have been the one to murder Jill; had something gone wrong on their date and the two got into a fight before he murdered her? Authorities looked into this scenario, but Brady had come straight home to the apartment he shared with a few roommates right after the game, and he was quickly ruled out as the suspect.

Things got worse in the area in the few days following Jill's death. On June 17, police responded to a call concerning Robyn Billingsley, a ten-year-old girl from Oxnard, who had been kidnapped when she was heading to the beach. Only a day later, Billingsley was found raped and beaten in an area between Malibu and Oxnard. Luckily, this little girl was still alive, although the scars would haunt her for a long time to come.

At the same time, two boys were found in this same area. The bodies were found in the Oxnard area, and the attacker had sexually molested both children. After these three attacks, the residents of this area, and anywhere near it, went on high alert. They felt that a serial murderer was on the loose and pressured authorities to find out who was responsible.

All the while, Rodney Alcala was out in the open, enjoying the new life he had created. Instead of working the traditional nine to five job or being in jail where he belonged, he was out taking pictures and enjoying the beautiful scenery that was around him. The thoughts of his pending trial seemed to be the furthest thing from his mind.

At the same time, authorities from New York were working to connect Alcala to the Hover case. While most authorities believed that Alcala was the one to blame for Hover's death, they weren't able to find enough hard evidence to link him to the case. Alcala had done an excellent job of cleaning up the scene, and it still wasn't possible to use any DNA testing to see who had been at the scene. Investigators were still suspicious of Alcala and felt that they would soon stumble upon something to link this man to the death of Hover.

June - 1979

Alcala seemed to have a lot of free time once authorities released him from jail after the Hoyt incident. His mother had taken care of the bail issue, ensuring that he wouldn't be out any money if he never showed up to jail. Alcala also quit his job to pursue his photography business, so he didn't even have his job to keep him busy at this time.

For a man who had trouble staying out of mischief even when he was busy, and one who felt that he was able to get away with anything, this was not a real scenario. And of course, during this time, more attacks occurred.

On June 19, 1979, Joanne Murchland, fourteen, and Toni Esparza, fifteen, were out on the beach near Orange County. This area was a beautiful stretch of land, one of the longest beaches in the area, and the two were spending some time after lunch roller skating in the area.

All of a sudden, they were approached by a man in a car. He seemed friendly enough, and they started to talk to him. After a few minutes, he introduced himself as a photography student and asked if they would mind doing a quick photo shoot. The young girls felt flattered that this charming man would pay them any attention. The man went on to explain that there was a prize involved for the picture that won. The girls noticed that the man had a nice looking camera and some equipment and felt that his story checked out. They decided to take some pictures for the man.

The man got out of the car and had the girls skate around the pier a bit. He gave a few directions onto how he would like them to move. They spent some time doing different poses so that he could get all the pictures that he needed. After doing quite a few with the girls together, the man asked to take just a few shots of Joanne before finishing up. Before the man headed off, he asked the two girls for their numbers so he could give them a call if the pictures won the contest.

Feeling that something was off, Toni said she would not give out her phone number, but Joanne hesitated a bit. The man then asked them for their addresses to see if he could send them information later on. These questions raised an even bigger red flag to Toni, and she grabbed Joanne's hand and the two left as fast as they could from the area.

The next day, on June 20, another victim met this strange photography student. Lorraine Werts, a fifteen-year-old girl, was spending some time at Sunset Beach with a new friend she had just met at school, Patty Elmendorf. After some time, the two were skating back to the bus stop to go home, when Elmendorf stopped to go to the bathroom and promised to be right back.

The second that Elmendorf skated to the bathroom, a strange man came up to Werts. He used a story similar to what he had explained to the girls the day before; how he was a photography student trying to win a contest. Werts had always wanted to get into modeling and felt flattered that this man was interested in her pictures. She figured this could be her big break and agreed to take some photos. After the man had taken a few, he started asking some personal questions, such as where Werts lived. She felt something was off, and as soon as she saw Elmendorf come from the bathroom, the two left right away.

Robin Samsoe - 1979

Later that day, two twelve-year-old girls, Bridget Wilvert, and Robin Samsoe headed off to Huntington Beach. While the two girls were at the beach, a man who had a large camera around his neck approached them. He asked if he could take their picture because he loved how they looked playing in the sand. The two girls felt flattered and agreed to take the photos.

A short distance away, another person, Jackie Young noticed that a weirdly dressed man had approached these girls, and she felt that something was off. Young headed over to this group and recognized Wilvert as her neighbor. When Young approached to say hi, the man got nervous and headed away.

Later that day, Samsoe didn't show up to a ballet class that she helped to run. The ballet teacher, Fleming, called Samsoe's home and asked if Samsoe was on her way over. After calling around, Samsoe's aunt when to talk to Wilvert, whom she knew had been with Samsoe earlier that day. Wilvert claimed that Samsoe had borrowed her bike a little after three that afternoon and left to go to the ballet school. Samsoe's family called around to some of her friends, but no one else had seen the young girl all day.

By that night, they were becoming worried that something had happened to their daughter. They called the police in the hopes that someone would be able to help them. News about this disappearance went public quickly as the local television channels showed the composite drawing. This picture showed a curly haired man and came out about the same time that Alcala decided to straighten out his curly hair.

On June 26, after authorities spent a lot of time questioning people on the beach, the started looking through their registry of past perpetrators. When they got to the picture of Alcala, most of them agreed that he fit the profile and looked a lot like the composite sketch. Alcala soon became a person of interest. Considering he had a criminal record already in place for kidnapping in that area, authorities felt that he could be the one.

Authorities sprung into action. They picked out six pictures from their lineup, all of which had similar looks to the composite sketch, and included Alcala's picture. Then authorities brought in all who had come forward claiming that an unknown photographer had tried to take their picture around the time that Samsoe disappeared. All of them picked Alcala's picture out of the lineup.

Authorities found Robin Samsoe on June 29 and identified her after the 4th of July Holiday on July 6. They used an autopsy and dental records to prove who this young girl was. Since so much time had passed since her death, it was uncertain what had caused her to die.

The Investigation into Samsoe's Death

It wasn't until authorities accused Alcala of killing Robin Samsoe that he was finally stopped. There were several witnesses who talked to Alcala in the few days before Samsoe disappeared and one of Samsoe's friends identified Alcala as a man who had tried to take their pictures. Alcala went to jail and awaited trial.

Over time, Alcala had seemed to be incapable of staying out of trouble. He had gotten used to being able to get away with these crimes without ever having to pay for it. But by the time investigators found the remains of twelve-year-old Samsoe, they felt that they finally had him.

Investigators had been able to go off tips from two police officers, the fact that Alcala had been paroled for this kind of infraction in the past that several witnesses had picked out Alcala's picture from a lineup and that Alcala looked like the composite image. Seeing the composite made the investigators feel like they may have caught their man.

On July 24, the police arrived at the home of Alcala's mother with a warrant to search the home as well as the station wagon that Alcala had been using. They arrived at the home early that morning and were allowed in by Alcala's mother. Alcala was in his bed, naked, but was allowed to get dressed while the police handcuffed him and moved him to headquarters so police could interview him. The first piece of evidence that investigators found was a receipt for a locker that was purchased right after Samsoe disappeared. Some other evidence that police collected that day include:

- Eight copies of "Young and Naked"

- Pieces of rope
- Envelopes containing mail
- Boxes of photos
- One pair of handcuffs
- 1,200 photos, slides, and negatives
- A briefcase with some keys
- Various camera equipment
- One pair NBA running shoes
- One plaid men's shirt
- One leather bullwhip
- One black wig
- Plastic slide tray and other slides
- Two photo binders

Alcala claimed that he had been at an interview on the day in question, but police still felt he was the one that committed this murder. They were able to get the bail set at $250,000.

Alcala's family went into action the next day. Alcala's sister offered an alibi for Alcala, stating that he had been babysitting her kids for most of the day in question. Also, his mother showed authorities a phone bill that listed a forty-minute phone call from her home to Alcala's girlfriend's home. Even though there was a bit of information to help out Alcala, investigators were interested in learning more about the locker Alcala had rented.

So on July 26, they got a search warrant, and two of the investigators headed to the storage unit. The officers noticed that this unit had two padlocks, but they were able to open it using the keys that came with the confiscated briefcase. There were various objects in the locker including a red coin purse, various jewelry, and more than 1,700 photographs, slides, and negatives. The two items that stood out the most to the investigators included one called "Ode to New York by John Berger" and "Tali VA Rape."

Trial, Conviction, and Sentencing

The multiple trials of Rodney Alcala were complicated. There were many murders, and the investigations into each went on at different times throughout the years. For his first trial for the attack on Tali Shapiro, he was let off with lesser charges thanks to his victim being out of the country and unwilling to come back to speak out against Rodney. Later trials would not go as smoothly for Alcala.

On July 28, Alcala was arraigned for the murder of Robin Samsoe, the twelve-year-old girl he had kidnapped and killed after she had posed for him. Alcala pled that he was innocent of all the charges brought against him, and his preliminary hearing was set for August 9.

This time Alcala was held without bail. Alcala requested that the judge provide him with a public defender; the judge granted this after considering that Alcala didn't have a job or any means to afford one. If they convicted Alcala of this murder, he could face the death penalty in California.

At the time, Alcala was still facing a trial in Riverside County for raping and assaulting Monique Hoyt back in February.

The first public defender assigned to Alcala was replaced with another defender right away. Alcala had made confessions about this crime to a few of the inmates; these inmates were clients of the public defender and presented a conflict of interest if the defender kept working with Alcala. The court placed John Barnett on the case and he quickly asked for more time before the trial so that he could study the case.

The preliminary hearing for this trial occurred in September of 1979. The biggest issue at present was whether the judge would allow Alcala's prior offenses to be admissible in the court; if they were admissible, this would make it more difficult for Alcala to get a favorable outcome.

The judge, Philip E. Schwab decided that the prior offenses would be allowed in court and that decision proved to be an enormous victory for the prosecution. Many felt that this is what Alcala deserved. After years of the justice system taking it easy on him, and allowing for so many more people to die, it was time for him to face some justice.

The day of the proceedings was big in the area. The story of young Samsoe's death, as well as the many others this same man had approached that day, brought people in from all over to follow the trial. Probably the most riveting witness at the time was Dana Crappa. She thought she saw something on the day that Samsoe was murdered but had brushed it aside thinking it was nothing to worry about at the time. Whether she couldn't remember what had occurred or was worried that she would get in trouble for not reporting her information earlier, her story had changed many times during the investigation and by the trial in 1980, it was undetermined which way she would go with the story.

There was also a lot of other evidence presented. Several inmates who had spent time with Alcala stated that Alcala had talked about what happened to Robin while in prison. The prosecutors also pointed out that Alcala had a history of luring women into his car before harming them, either sexually, or by murdering them, or a combination. It was a tense few days in the courtroom as each side tried to prove their point to the jurors.

On April 29, 1980, the jurors went into deliberations. Interested parties on both sides were holding their breaths for the answer. There wasn't any verdict on that first day. On April 30, the jurors finally reached their decision. The jurors found Alcala guilty of first-degree murder with the use of a deadly weapon as well as guilty of forcible kidnapping.

The penalty phase of the trial ended on May 7 of 1980, and the jurors were given the case the next day. After about four hours of weighing the case, the jurors made their decision. The jurors all sentenced Alcala to death. The judge stated that the sentencing would be carried out on July 20, 1980, precisely a year after Samsoe's death.

Other Trials Against Alcala

On July 11, right after the judge had signed for the death sentence on Alcala, the District Attorney's office in Los Angeles filed charges of sexual assault, burglary, and murder against Alcala in the killing of Jill Parenteau. This crime had occurred less than a week before Samsoe's death, and it was considered a special circumstance case; this meant that the prosecution would be seeking the death sentence. The key point that linked Alcala to this murder is the blood types that were found in the area. The first blood type was Jill's; the other matched very closely to Alcala's.

Apparently, Alcala and Jill had met at a bar. Alcala showed a lot of interest in Jill, but she did not feel the same way. Once Jill rebuffed Alcala, she began to receive some obscene phone calls from the man. The authorities matched these calls with Alcala's location; whenever he was in the area, he would bug Jill, but when he left the area, these calls would stop. Prosecutors alleged that Alcala had broken into Jill's apartment before beating, raping, and strangling her to death.

Alcala never went to trial for the murder of Jill. The inmate John Mulqueen, who had been a crucial witness in this case, was linked to lying in another case when he was a principal witness. Since the primary witness had lied in the past, he was no longer a credible witness and could not testify for the prosecutors against Alcala. Because of this, the case against Parenteau and Alcala was dismissed from the courts.

By September 1980, Alcala was brought to stand trial for his part in the 1979 rape and beating of Monique Hoyt. This trial took place despite the fact that Alcala was already sentenced to die for his murder of Samsoe.

During this trial, officials from Riverside County came in to testify about the facts surrounding this case. They talked about how Alcala had picked up Hoyt on February 13, 1979, and how she was able to escape and reach the authorities. Hoyt had also been able to identify her attacker.

This trial was much shorter than the last one. In the end, Alcala was pronounced guilty of rape in the Hoyt case. During the penalty phase of this trial, the prosecution played the recorded interview that Alcala had given to authorities after the Hoyt incident. Between this, and the before and after pictures they found in Alcala's possession, Alcala knew it would be worthless to try and defend himself, and he confessed to causing harm to Hoyt while confirming her story. The jury gave Alcala the sentence of nine years in prison for this rape.

Despite being given the death sentence for his murder of Robin Samsoe, Alcala, and his appeals attorney decided to appeal this decision. Keith Monroe worked with Alcala eight months after the verdict, to help free Alcala. They worked on two grievances with the original trial. Monroe stated that the first issue was that too much weight had been given to the testimony of the jail informants. There was also the issue that the prosecution rejected several jurors because they didn't agree with using a death sentence, something that was not allowed by federal law.

The appeals process gripped the people in LA for five days, starting on April 10, 1981. While the appeals lawyer believed that the testimony from the inmates should be thrown out and this would remove Alcala, many believed that there was enough evidence to put Alcala away even without it.

When brought before the judge, one of the inmates confessed that he had lied during the trial about hearing Alcala talk about the murder of Samsoe. The fact that one of the witnesses lied had a lot of bearing on the case. Without this testimony, there was no proof or evidence that Alcala had even kidnapped Samsoe, meaning that he would not be eligible for the death.

On May 28, 1981, the judge ruled whether the case for Samsoe would be dismissed based on the inmate testimony. If the judge ruled that the prisoner told the truth in his testimony, the kidnapping charges would not be dismissed, and Alcala still faced the death sentence. If they determined that the witness lied during the trial, then the kidnapping charge against Alcala would be dropped.

The judge ruled against Alcala, and he was returned to death row at San Quentin. While Samsoe's friends and family were elated, Monroe stated that he would go to the California Supreme Court to appeal this decision.

Alcala spent the next three years in a cell at San Quentin. Then on August 23, 1984, the California Supreme Court wrote their decision on the appeal of Alcala's death sentence. The court ruled that Alcala would not undergo the death sentence. They felt that the original court had made a mistake in allowing Alcala's past crimes to be revealed in court; a mistake that led the jurors to already feel prejudiced against Alcala before the trial even began. All but one juror believed that the prior crimes were not similar enough to this present one to be taken into consideration in the 1980 trial.

While this was great news for Alcala, there was a catch. The defense for Alcala had hoped he would be saved by the double jeopardy clause so he would not stand another trial for this case. The courts did not support this though, and Alcala would still have to face another trial for the death of Samsoe, although this time the courts could not bring in the past crimes of the defendant.

On April 23, 1986, Alcala went through his second trial, led by Judge Donald A. McCartin. This time, the prosecution had to try and bring up new evidence and testimonies to get Alcala back in jail. Since there was no evidence that directly linked him to the crime physically, they tried to get as many of the witnesses back into the courtroom as possible; this was difficult after seven years.

One break they got was from a new inmate that had spent some time in jail with Alcala after he was sentenced. This inmate described how Alcala had laughed about the case and how the authorities were missing out on important bits of the puzzle and how they all looked silly for doing it.

It took four days for the jurors to come back with a verdict this time. On May 28, the jurors agreed that Alcala was guilty on the accounts of murder, false imprisonment, and the special circumstances of the kidnapping that led to the murder. On June 9, before the penalty phase began, Alcala submitted a document to the judge stating that he thought his case should be dismissed because his lawyers had not provided him with an adequate defense. The judge denied this request.

After hearing evidence, the jurors decided on the death sentence for Alcala. The judge decided to go with a formal sentencing that would be set on August 20. In California, it was possible for the judge to change the sentencing of death over to a life in prison without parole if they saw fit.

On August 20, 1986, Alcala went back to court. Before handing down the judgment on Alcala, Judge McCartin spent some time going down some of the most horrific parts of Alcala's history starting way back in 1968. When this was done, Judge McCartin stated: "It is clear that nothing in Alcala's past has made an impression on Mr. Alcala." To end it out, McCartin agreed with the death penalty for the kidnapping and killing of Robin Samsoe.

Alcala was sent back to San Quentin to wait on death row, but he would be waiting for the automatic appeal that came with his death sentence. Alcala spent the next few years in prison, waiting to find out what the Supreme Court in California would say about the conviction. It seemed that Alcala was not worried about the results. He was interviewed during this time and often stated how he was comfortable in the new spot, was able to watch TV and do other activities, and how he did not think there was anything to worry about when it came to the death penalty. California had not given out this punishment in some time, and Alcala felt that now would not be the time they made changes to this.

It wasn't until December 31, 1992, that the court affirmed the conviction as well as the death sentence from Alcala's 1986 trial. The court did acknowledge that there were a few errors that were made during the guilt phase of this trial, but the errors were seen as harmless and not important to the outcome of the trial.

They also determined that Alcala had received a trial that was untainted and fair and that there was nothing else required for the courts. With this verdict Alcala would still stay on death row, waiting until the state puts him to death.

It seemed that finally Alcala had run out of luck. He had been avoiding the law for years, going from his first case of beating and raping a young girl (for which he got off with a much lesser charge since she and her family moved out of the country and refused to come back), to the Hoyt case where the girl was able to recognize him and the Samsoe case that sent him to jail. It took the courts years, and perhaps they should have caught Alcala beforehand if he hadn't been allowed to roam free so many times. But now, it looked like Alcala was going to pay for his bad deeds and face the death penalty.

Current Status

Alcala was not executed right away, although he stayed in prison on death row for some time. Over the course of the next few years, Alcala kept busy with writing his personal story. Alcala still believed that he was innocent, saying that he had never harmed those girls or that something had been wrong with his trial. So during his time on death row, Alcala wrote a book, over three hundred pages, under the publishing house of Buquor Books of Fremont, California. This book was called *"You, the Jury"*.

This book was meant to help out Alcala's case by espousing that he was not supposed to be on death row at all. Alcala tried to get people to be the jury by reading his book. He spelled out the different pieces of evidence given during his trial and asked readers to determine what they thought should be the outcome. Alcala did this because he felt that he had been the one wronged in the system. He felt that others would agree with him. The book was published in 1994 and messed up quite a few of the facts now known about the beatings and murders.

For example, Alcala spent some time talking about the murder of Robin Samsoe. He claimed that he was innocent in this murder and had nothing to do with it. Alcala then goes on to say how no one knew the reason that Samsoe left her home in Huntington Beach and headed to an abandoned spot in the mountains. He then finished with how he had never even met Robin and had nothing to do with her murder. Of course, these facts had been proven wrong at several trials, but Alcala was still maintaining that he was innocent and had been put on death row unjustly.

Most people felt that this was just Alcala's way of trying to dupe the people or perhaps get off death row. While there was some information about the case within the book, there was a lot of extra fluff that was not all that relevant. For example, most of the book was filled with footnotes and the book included an extensive survey that readers should fill out about this book. And of course, it was easy to send back to receive another book with the handy form found in the original copy.

Alcala spent quite a bit of time in prison waiting for death row. It was more than nine years before anything else was heard about this case again. In March of 2001, the higher court handed out a reversal to Alcala's conviction on the second trial. This court determined that the sentence handed out in the second trial should be overturned.

There were two major things that helped to reverse this case. First, the higher court decided that it was a huge error that Dana Crappa was not brought back out to talk about what she had seen at the time of the murder. In the second trial, Crappa was not brought back in, but her testimony from the first trial was read out to the jury.

The second issue is that the judge decided not to allow a psychologist to testify on the side of the defense. The particular doctor, Ray William London, had spent some time listening to the tapes of Crappa during the first trial, and during her testimonies, and felt that Crappa had been induced to give her account and that the statements may be false. The judge at the second trial never let this psychologist speak up for the defense.

Because of these, and the fact that the defense for Alcala never used a witness to show that Alcala had been at a job interview at the time of Samsoe's murder, the court concluded that Alcala should be either released from custody, or he should be allowed to have a retrial over the case.

The mood for this decision went both ways. Some people, such as the family members of Alcala, felt that this was justice. They had long stood by the side of their brother, even though he had past convictions that supported this kind of behavior, and stated that he was innocent. They felt that Alcala finally had a chance to be free and live his normal life.

Others, such as Samsoe's mother and the judge who had ruled at the second trial, felt that this was completely insane. They knew they had lined up the evidence correctly, and that Alcala was the man they were looking for. Samsoe's mother decided to take a different approach. She felt that people had heard enough about Alcala over the years and that he had taken enough of her time and energy. Instead, she tried to switch around public support by talking about her daughter and the amazing person Robin had been before she died.

The higher court gave the state of California up to 120 days to release or retry Alcala for his crime. The state, feeling that this ruling had been done incorrectly, contacted the Ninth Circuit Court of Appeals to see if they were able to get a reversal of their judgment.

During 2002, there were some changes allowed in many criminal cases. Corrections officers and law enforcement were allowed to take samples of DNA from the prisoners and could even use force that was reasonable if the prisoner would not give up the sample voluntarily. Once the DNA was obtained, the investigators would enter it into a database, which would be expanded over time as more samples came in, to search for the profiles of DNA that would match evidence at a crime scene. What was great about this is that the DNA could be attached to newer as well as cold cases.

Allowing DNA evidence was a huge decision that was passed by the state. It allowed law enforcement officials to compare DNA from various crime scenes with the DNA of their prisoners. The hope was this would help the police to solve some of their cases.

Alcala had always been against this new program. While it was going through the state, he often spoke out about how unfair this was and that prisoners should not have to submit their DNA. He felt that the justice system should do a good enough job at all this that the DNA sample would not be necessary.

When it came to Alcala's third trial in 2003, this new procedure would start to work against him. Investigators began to put Alcala's name to many of the murders that he had committed. At the time, Alcala had only faced trial for a few of them. No one was able to link him to any of the others. But once DNA was allowed in court cases and for matching criminals with some of these cases, things began to turn for Alcala.

Matt Murphy was the first one to find out about another murder that Alcala had committed. Murphy was the senior Deputy DA in Orange County and had been placed on the Alcala case. One day while he was getting the information set up for the trial, he received a call from the DA in Los Angeles County. The DNA testing and database had linked Alcala up to the death of Wixted, the 1977 murder in Malibu. The semen that Alcala had left behind during the rape was connected back to him.

Because of the DNA link, the DA's office in Los Angeles filed charges of murder against Alcala in June of 2003. This was going to be the first case that linked Alcala to a murder. The others had been circumstantial, part of the reason that Alcala had been able to walk away free and avoid the death sentence at this time. This particular charge of murder not only alleged that Alcala had killed Georgia Wixted, but that he had also raped and committed burglary. All these charges put Alcala into eligibility for a special circumstances case. If Alcala were convicted, he could face the death sentence again.

The DA offices in Los Angeles and Orange County started to work together. They both had information on Alcala and wanted to find out just how far this man had gone with some of the cold cases of the time. Working together, the two offices went through all their cold case files that started back in the 1970s. They began with any that matched the Wixted case, feeling that Alcala may have been involved in these as well.

While investigators were working on linking Alcala to some other murders in the area, Alcala received some good news. Although the state of California had tried to repeal the higher courts reversal of the death sentence, the higher court upheld their decision. This ruling meant that Alcala could walk free again if the local court were not able to come up with a strong enough case to retry Alcala.

Samsoe's family felt that it was all lost. A third trial would be difficult. A lot of time had passed over the years, and even eyewitnesses will find that their memories of the event will fail. It is easier for the defense to question that witness about little things, things that the person is going to have trouble remembering exactly over the years. No matter how small these parts may be, it can often be enough to put a reasonable doubt in the minds of the jury. Many worried that Alcala was going to walk free.

Alcala met with Francisco Pedro Briseno, the court judge for this third trial, on October 7, 2003. Alcala pled not guilty to this crime again and then asked the judge if he would be able to act as a lawyer in this trial. Alcala talked about how he had spent some time reviewing the information in the trial and felt that he would

71

be able to assist another lawyer in his defense. Briseno agreed to this request. The trial was not set to start until 2005.

Even though Alcala had some time before his third trial for the death of Robin Samsoe, investigators were still looking for DNA evidence that could link him to other crimes in the area. In 2004, there was another DNA match found. This time, the DNA matched Alcala with the death of Jill Barcomb. This death was one that had shocked many investigators. For years, they had believed that Barcomb was another victim from the Hillside Strangler, but this new DNA evidence showed that Alcala was the one responsible.

Now with three murders, that of Samsoe, Wixted, and Barcomb, Alcala had been elevated to a serial killer. Two more victims showed up before long, including Charlotte Lamb, a secretary who was murdered in 1978 and Jill Parenteau. The count was now up to five and things were not looking good for Alcala, no matter what happened with his third trial.

Investigators were shocked to find out how many murders involved Alcala. They felt that the only reason these deaths had stopped was because Alcala was finally placed behind bars and had not been allowed out since 1979. The investigators from Orange County and Los Angeles County began to work on a case against Alcala in these new murders.

The investigators were interested in putting all five of these deaths into one case. Alcala's lawyer was not so fond of the idea, feeling that having the jury listen to all of the cases would prejudice the jury against Alcala in the Samsoe case and wouldn't provide Alcala with a fair trial.

On May 25, 2006, Briseno agreed that all five murders could be consolidated into one trial. Despite this declaration and the fact that prosecutors had some DNA evidence to help them make a case, the trial still did not happen until 2007. In fact, Alcala had appealed the one trial and asked the district courts to intervene. Alcala was able to get two trials. There would be one trial for the Samsoe, Lamb, and Parenteau cases and one for the Wixted and Barcomb cases. This decision was again reversed in 2008 when the Supreme Court of California ruled that all of the cases should have the same trial.

Before the trial could go on, Alcala began to fight the justice system in the hopes of being allowed to act as his own lawyer in the case. Briseno disagreed, saying that Alcala should allow someone else to be his lawyer. This would give Alcala a chance later to appeal saying his attorney hadn't done a good job, but if Alcala represented himself, this was no longer a possibility. Despite being turned down by Briseno multiple times, Alcala finally won when the district court of the area allowed Alcala to represent himself.

The third trial finally happened on January 11, 2010. This ended up being a long trial that continued until February 22. Alcala's defense did not go well. He brought out an ex-girlfriend to support his case, used his video from the Dating Game to try and show he had golden earrings before the victim died, and even interviewed himself. While interviewing himself, Alcala used a deeper than normal tone for the voice of the interviewer and his own normal voice to answer the questions. This brought an almost surreal cast over the whole proceedings. Finally, on February 23, deliberations for this case began.

The jury came back on the 25th with their verdict. The verdict was not what Alcala wanted to hear. The jury found that Alcala was guilty on the counts of five murders. Alcala was also convicted of five allegations that were considered special circumstances including kidnapping, multiple murder, rape, and torture. Alcala could yet again be eligible for the death sentence. On March 9, 2010, the jury decided to give Alcala capital punishment for the above crimes. On March 30, 2010, Briseno agreed with the charges and did not offer Alcala life without the possibility of parole.

While he was waiting on death row, Alcala was also linked up to the death of those he had killed in New York. The DNA evidence showed that he had been involved in murders all throughout the country, even though no one had tried to stop him when authorities did catch him. The jury indicted Alcala for the killings of Crilley and Hover in 2011 and then sentenced him to 25 years minimum in prison for these murders in 2013. At this time, Alcala is still awaiting death on death row in California for the murders he committed there.

During these trials, authorities decided to release the pictures they had found in the possession of Alcala. Most of these were the same, showing girls and boys in provocative stances and without wearing their clothes. These were many of the same pictures that Alcala had proudly shown off when he worked for the Los Angeles Time. Authorities hoped that by showing these images, they would be able to figure out some more of the cold cases on their hands. They asked individuals to respond if they had any idea who the people in the pictures were.

Some have come forward. Some of these were the victims who were then able to testify against Alcala and state what had gone on. Many were the families of other cold case victims; these families had long given up hope of ever finding out what happened to their loved ones. While these pictures were disturbing, these families were able to find some closure knowing who had been the one responsible for these deaths.

While there are some investigations going on to find the bodies of some of these individuals and to promote a stronger case for Alcala in case he does get out of jail again, these are still, in the beginning, phases. Until investigators can figure out where the bodies have gone and use DNA evidence to link Alcala to these deaths, it might be some time before these can go to trial as well as the others.

At the very least, releasing these pictures helped investigators to see the full extent of what Alcala was up to all those years. There are many cases that had stymied investigators and were later able to point back to Alcala. Even though there is a lot of evidence against Alcala in regards to these murders, Alcala still maintains that he is innocent and did not kill any of the women. Professionals who have studied the case feel that this is due to the mental illness that no one helped Alcala fix. Alcala can separate out the events that occur in his life. He may feel that another part of him, perhaps another person in him, was the one who committed the murders while he was just an innocent bystander.

At this time, Alcala is still waiting on death row for his sentencing to be carried out. The families and loved ones of the women he killed are looking forward to the day that this man finally gets the end that he deserves.

Conclusion

The story of Rodney Alcala has fascinated people for years. Alcala was a man who had a lot of charisma and brains and was able to make almost anyone feel comfortable around him. But despite this, he had troubles from an early age. Before leaving the Army as a young man, he had been diagnosed with some mental issues that influenced the way that Alcala saw the world. Since his discharge, he did not receive the care that he needed for these disorders, and this might have been why he was allowed to keep on with his current life.

Rodney was smart and able to keep away from authorities for a long time. He decided to go to college shortly after being released from the Army and did well there. He made some friends, and everyone liked being around him. But during this time, the mental disorders were not being treated. In fact, they seemed to get worse until Rodney attacked Tali Shapiro, beating her and raping her. Luckily, this young woman lived since someone had followed them and was able to intervene. Unfortunately, Shapiro and her family had moved out of the country and refused to come back for a trial. Without Shapiro, the primary witness for the prosecution was gone, and they were forced to agree to a lesser guilty plea bargain with Rodney once authorities brought him back from New York where he had been studying film and working as a camp counselor.

Alcala was able to work the system well. At the time, the state of California had a rehabilitation program in place. This program worked by allowing prisoners to get out of jail early if they worked with the psychologist and showed improvement. Alcala got out for this first crime in just a few months before heading out and causing trouble again. This time, Alcala had been found giving marijuana to a minor while he was on parole and he went back to jail. Knowing how the system worked again, this time, Alcala was able to get out of jail in less than two years.

It seemed like Alcala was quiet for some time after these occurrences. Since there wasn't the ability to use DNA evidence at the time, Alcala was able to get away with quite a few murders and rapes before anyone caught him for anything. There were several times that investigators came to talk to Alcala, but he pretended to have no idea what they were talking about and usually could talk his way out of trouble.

When Alcala finally did get caught for the Samsoe case, it would take years for much to happen. Through a lot of appeals processes, Alcala ended up having three trials for this one case. Two of them were just for the Samsoe girl, and another was for Samsoe as well as four other young women that Alcala had murdered. Unfortunately, these were not the only killings and attacks; Alcala was also convicted of kidnapping and harming Hoyt and was indicted and sentenced for a 25 year minimum for two other murders he had committed in New York.

For the third and final trial, the one that had five different cases against Alcala and DNA evidence to back it up, Alcala decided to be his own defense attorney. Though the courts tried to convince him this was a bad idea, Alcala went ahead with the plan. This idea ended up badly, putting Alcala in some awkward situations, such as interviewing himself, and the jury sentenced him to death for killing these five women.

Over the years, the media started calling Alcala the Dating Game Killer. While he had never killed anyone through this television show, he was once on it and had been the winner at the time. Alcala spent quite a few years in prison, from 1979 when authorities first caught him until the present day, and the media still liked to pull up videos of his time on the Dating Game when discussing the Alcala case.

Many feel that the justice system should have been able to do more to keep this man behind bars. There were many murders and attempted murders that were eventually associated with Alcala thanks to DNA testing that had become usable a few years after Alcala went to jail. Many law enforcement professionals who worked on these cases feel that the only reason Alcala stopped murdering his victims is that he is behind bars.

So why was Alcala allowed to run free for all this time? Why hadn't he received the attention that he needed, the attention that was recognized way back during his time in the military? Alcala had a way of working with people. Although some knew that he needed help with his mental issues, Alcala was usually able to talk his way out of them. For example, Alcala was sentenced to two separate 10-year sentences for his attack on Shapiro and for offering marijuana to a minor. And yet he served less than five years total because he was able to work with the local psychologist and was successful in convincing them that he was rehabilitated and ready to go back into society.

If Alcala had gotten the help that he deserved, or even if Shapiro had been able to testify at his first trial, it is likely that he would have stopped the killing spree much earlier on. Perhaps he would have gotten help before his need to kill took over. Or perhaps it would have all stopped once Alcala was permanently behind bars for harming Shapiro all those years ago. Even once he was in jail, there were plenty of times that things went favorably for Alcala. Many technicalities and other issues, at least until the DNA evidence came to light, helped to get Alcala out of harm's way and even though authorities put him in jail in 1979, he still has not faced his death sentence.

There are many serial murderers that have caught the attention of the mass public. These murderers seem to have a secret way of not getting caught for all the heinous things they have done over time. They are able to get away with countless murders, some just a few while others, like Alcala, were possibly up in the hundreds. These murderers sparked fear in many people of the area. These people would change their daily habits; refusing to walk alone to any place, never staying out past dark, and always being cautious when around a new person. Some of these murderers were never caught while others were able to get away with many killings before they were finally brought to justice.

Rodney Alcala was one of these cases. This man has fascinated people for years, especially since he showed such early signs of having mental disorders and needing the help of a professional. He never did get the help that he needed, simply being passed over from one person to the next. Even when he did get caught in jail, he was quickly released for knowing how to play the system. Ultimately, the system failed and many young women, of all ages and from across the country, ended up being killed by this man.

As you can see here, there is a lot that went on during the lifetime of Rodney Alcala. He committed many crimes and was able to walk free or talk his way out of many other crimes over the years. All the victims had trusted this man because he was easy to get along with and great at talking to others. It is a testament to the mind behind the serial killer, how he was able to get away with all of this for so long, and how getting Alcala some help from the beginning could have made it all so much better.

The photographs found in Rodney Alcala's locker are still on display on Flickr at
https://www.flickr.com/photos/scpr/sets/72157623600695928/

The authorities are still hoping family or friends of the people in the photos will recognize them and bring some closure to their cases.

Also by Jack Smith

WRONGFUL CONVICTIONS

TRUE MURDER CASES
UNBELIEVABLE MISCARRIAGES OF JUSTICE

JACK SMITH

BY PERSON OR PERSONS...

U N K N O W N

SHEDDING NEW LIGHT ON TRUE UNSOLVED MURDER
MYSTERIES LOST IN TIME BUT NEVER FORGOTTEN

JACK SMITH

DR. DEATH

Life of
Serial Killer
Michael
Swango

Jack Smith

THE HAPPY FACE MURDERER

The Life of Serial Killer Keith Hunter Jesperson

Jack Smith

THE HORRIFIC CRIMES GILLES DE RAIS REVISITED

Life of a Serial Killer of the Middle Ages
Jack Smith

THE BEAST OF BIRKENSHAW

LIFE OF SERIAL KILLER
PETER MANUEL

JACK SMITH

BODIES IN BARRELS

THE SNOWTOWN MURDERS

JACK SMITH

HIDDEN BRUTALITY

LIFE OF SERIAL KILLER CARL EUGENE WATTS

JACK SMITH

THE SPOKANE KILLER

The Life of Serial Killer Robert Lee Yates Jr

Jack Smith

Printed in Great Britain
by Amazon

50679995R00048